GALLUP GUIDES FOR YOUTH FACING PERSISTENT PREJUDICE

Asians

GALLUP GUIDES FOR YOUTH FACING PERSISTENT PREJUDICE

- Asians
- Blacks
- Hispanics
- Jews
- The LGBT Community
- Muslims
- Native North American Indians
- People with Mental and Physical Challenges

GALLUP GUIDES FOR YOUTH FACING PERSISTENT PREJUDICE

Asians

Z.B. Hill

Mason Crest

Mason Crest
370 Reed Road
Broomall, Pennsylvania 19008
www.masoncrest.com

Printed and bound in the United States of America.

First printing
9 8 7 6 5 4 3 2 1

ISBN-13: 978-1-4222-2462-5 (hardcover series)
ISBN-13: 978-1-4222-2463-2 (hardcover)
ISBN-13: 978-1-4222-9336-2 (e-book)

Library of Congress Cataloging-in-Publication Data

Hill, Z. B.
 Gallup guides for youth facing persistent prejudice. Asians / by Z.B. Hill.
    p. cm.
 Includes bibliographical references and index.
 ISBN 978-1-4222-2463-2 (hardcover) -- ISBN 978-1-4222-2462-5 (series hardcover) -- ISBN 978-1-4222-9336-2 (ebook)
 1. Asian Americans--Juvenile literature. 2. Prejudices--Juvenile literature. 3. Racism--Juvenile literature. I. Title. II. Title: Asians.
 E184.A75H55 2013
 305.8995'073--dc23

2012017107

Produced by Harding House Publishing Services, Inc.
www.hardinghousepages.com
Interior design by Micaela Sanna.
Page design elements by Cienpies Design / Illustrations | Dreamstime.com.
Cover design by Torque Advertising + Design.

CONTENTS

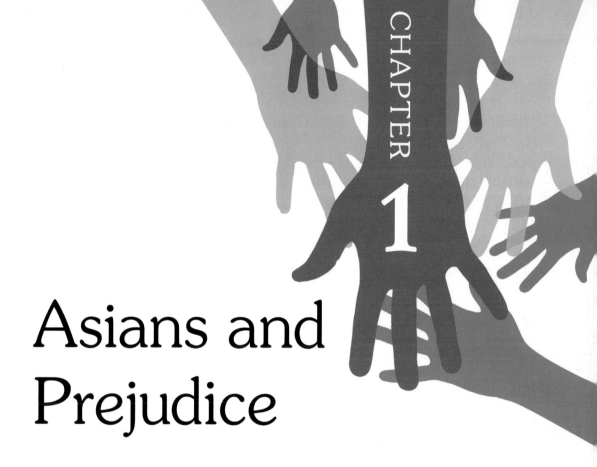

CHAPTER 1

Asians and Prejudice

E ver since the first Asians arrived in North America, they have struggled against anti-Asian prejudice. Over the course of 200 years, in both Canada and the United States, Asians have been denied equal rights. They have faced **harassment** and hostility. They've been imprisoned for no good reason, physically attacked, and even murdered.

WHAT IS PREJUDICE?

The root word of prejudice is "pre-judge." Prejudiced people often judge others based purely on their race, ethnic group, or religion; they make assumptions about others that may have no basis in reality. They believe that if your skin is a different color or you speak a different language or wear different clothes or worship God in a different way, then they already know you are not as smart, not as nice, not as honest, not as valuable, or not as moral as they are. Asians and Asian Americans have been the victims of prejudice for a long time in the United States.

Why do human beings experience prejudice? **Sociologists** believe humans have a basic tendency to fear anything that's unfamiliar or unknown. Someone who is strange (in that they're not like us) is scary; they're automatically dangerous

It's a human tendency to be cautious of the person who is different.

or inferior. If we get to know the strangers, of course, we end up discovering that they're not so different from ourselves. They're not so frightening and threatening after all. But too often, we don't let that happen. We put up a wall between the strangers and ourselves. We're on the inside; they're on the outside. And then we peer over the wall, too far away from the people on the other side to see anything but our differences. That's what has often happened when Asians and non-Asians interacted in the United States.

And here's where another human tendency comes into play: stereotyping.

STEREOTYPES

A stereotype is a fixed, commonly held idea or image of a person or group that's based on an **oversimplification** of some observed or imagined trait. Stereotypes assume that whatever is believed about a group is typical for each and every individual within that group. "All blondes are dumb," is a stereotype. "Women are poor drivers," is another. "Men are slobs," is yet another, and "Gay men are **effeminate**," is one as well.

Many stereotypes tend to make us feel superior in some way to the person or group being stereotyped. Not all stereotypes are negative, however; some are positive—"black men are good at basketball," "gay guys have good fashion sense," or "Asian students are smart"—but that doesn't make them true. They ignore individuals' uniqueness. They make assumptions that may or may not be accurate.

We can't help our human tendency to put people into categories. As babies, we faced a confusing world filled with an amazing variety of new things. We needed a way to make sense of it all, so one of our first steps in learning about the world around us was to sort things into separate slots in our heads: small furry things that said *meow* were kitties, while larger furry things that said *arf-arf* were doggies; cars went

High School Stereotypes

The average high school has its share of stereotypes—lumping a certain kind of person together, ignoring all the ways that each person is unique. These stereotypes are often expressed with a single word or phrase: "jock," "nerd," "goth," "prep," or "geek." The images these words call to mind are easily recognized and understood by others. But that doesn't mean they're true!

Group Pressure

Why do people continue to believe stereotypes despite evidence that may not support them? Researchers have found that it may have something to do with group pressure. During one experiment, seven members of a group were asked to state that a short line is longer than a long line. About a third of the rest of the group agreed that the short line was longer, despite evidence to the contrary. Apparently, people conform to the beliefs of those around them in order to gain group acceptance.

vroom-vroom, but trains were longer and went *choo-choo*; little girls looked one way and little boys another; and doctors wore white coats, while police officers wore blue. These were our earliest stereotypes. They were a handy way to make sense of the world; they helped us know what to expect, so that each time we faced a new person or thing, we weren't starting all over again from scratch.

But stereotypes become dangerous when we continue to hold onto our mental images despite new evidence. (For instance, as a child you may have decided that all dogs bite—which means that when faced by friendly, harmless dogs, you assume they're dangerous and so you miss out on getting to know all dogs.) Stereotypes are particularly dangerous and destructive when they're directed at persons or groups of persons. That's when they turn into prejudice.

There are several stereotypes aimed at Asian Americans. One is the "model minority" stereotype. People often think that all Asian Americans are well behaved, educated, and well-off. They don't contribute to crime, poverty, or other negative trends. Instead, they are the perfect sort of minority group. Besides assuming that all Asian Americans are the same, this stereotype ignores some of the problems that Asian American communities face, just like any other community.

Other Asian American stereotypes include thinking that all Asian Americans are smart, all Asian Americans are the same (for example, not realizing that Asian Americans come from a variety of different countries and backgrounds), and that all Asian Americans are weak and submissive.

RACISM

Prejudice and racism go hand-in-hand. Prejudice is an attitude, a way of looking at the world. When it turns into action it's called discrimination. Discrimination is when people are treated differently (and unfairly) because they belong to a particular group of people. Racism is a combination of the two. It's treating members of a certain "race" differently because you think they're not as good, simply because they belong to that race. You might say that prejudice is the root of racism—and discrimination is its branches and leaves.

There's one other concept that's important to racism as well—the belief that human beings can be divided into groups that are truly separate and different from one another. One

People often notice differences rather than similarities—when actually, all humans are more alike than they are different.

group that we think of as a race are Asians. Scientists aren't convinced, however, that we can really make these sorts of divisions.

A lot of the time, racism is built on words that don't have firm definitions. Think about the word "Asian." It covers a lot of different people. People in the United States and Canada might think of Chinese, Japanese, or Korean people when they hear the word "Asian." They're thinking of people from Eastern Asia. But technically, the category of Asian also includes people from other parts of Asia, like the southeastern region. Vietnamese, Cambodians, Laotians, and others are all Asian. So are people from India. And then there are the fuzzy borders. Where does Asia end? Most of Russia is in Asia. Does that make Russians Asian? What about people from the Middle East? Middle Easterners might not look like other people we consider to be Asian, but they technically live in Asia. As you can see, it's not so easy to define races!

When it comes down to it, scientifically, people are more alike than they're different, no matter what color their skin is or what continent their ancestors came from. In fact, scientists tell us that the idea of race is pretty much only useful as a medical concept—some groups of people from various parts

Prejudice Starts Inside

Sociologists have found that people who are prejudiced toward one group of people also tend to be prejudiced toward other groups. In a study done in 1946, people were asked about their attitudes concerning a variety of ethnic groups, including Danireans, Pirraneans, and Wallonians. The study found that people who were prejudiced toward blacks and Jews also distrusted these other three groups. The catch is that Danireans, Pirraneans, and Wallonians didn't exist! This suggests that prejudice's existence may be rooted within the person who feels prejudice rather than in the group that is feared and hated.

of the world are more likely to get some illnesses than others, and some may respond better to certain medications. This has to do with the **genes** that people tend to share if their ancestors come from the same place. **Sickle cell disease**, for example, is usually found among people whose ancestors lived in Africa or the Mediterranean region. **Cystic fibrosis** is more common among people whose ancestors came from

Six Characteristics of a Racial Minority Group

1. Minority group members suffer oppression at the hands of another group.

2. A minority group is identified by certain traits that are clearly visible and obvious.

3. Minorities see themselves as belonging to a special and separate social unit; they identify with others like themselves.

4. A person does not voluntarily become a member of a minority; he or she is born into it.

5. Members of racial minority groups usually don't marry outside the group. If intermarriage is high, ethnic identities and loyalties are weakening.

6. "Minority" is a social, not a numerical concept. In other words, it doesn't matter how many members of a particular "out-group" live in a region compared to the "in-group"; what matters are who has the power and social prestige.

Ethnocentrism

Ethnocentrism refers to a tendency to view one's own ethnic group's behaviors as "normal." Other groups are not only viewed as different, but they are seen as strange and sometimes inferior.

Europe. People descended from Africans don't always respond as well to certain kinds of heart medicines.

But people of all races are just as likely to be smart. They are just as trustworthy and kind, just as moral and hardworking.

In North America, some Asians get in trouble with the law—and so do some whites. Many Asians have problems. So do many whites.

Racism tells lies. Prejudice is one of those lies.

A History Lesson

P eople from Asia have been in North America for a very long time. Unfortunately, prejudice against Asians and Asian Americans has been around for almost the same amount of time.

EARLY IMMIGRANTS AND EARLY PREJUDICE

The first modern Asian people that are recorded to have lived in North American were a group of Chinese in Mexico. In the early 1600s, Chinese sailors decided to make their home in

The Very First Asians in North America

Technically, the first people from Asia came to what is today Canada and the United States a very, very long time ago. Thousands of years ago, many historians believe that people traveled across the Bering Land Strait from the northern-most tip of Russia into Alaska. Then they spread down into the rest of North, Central, and South America. They became Native North Americans—but they may have originally came from Asia!

Mexico, which was on their trading routes. Already, they faced discrimination, as other Mexicans asked that they be forced to live outside Mexico City rather than in its heart.

Later, other sailors from the Philippines made their way to present-day Louisiana. The first record of them dates from 1763. Their descendents still live there today.

But these were small communities. The first big wave of Asian immigrants came to North America during the California Gold Rush. News of the discovery of gold traveled all around

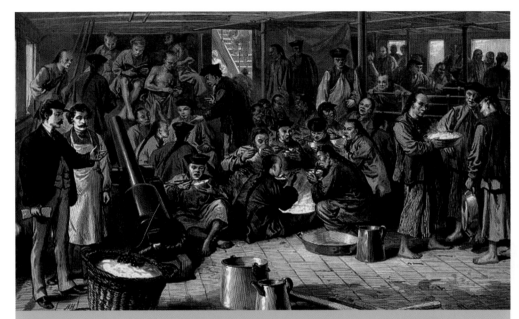

Large groups of people from China began immigrating to North America in the 1800s.

the United States. It reached all the way across the ocean, too. People in China heard about "Gold Mountain," an area where gold was lying around for the taking. Many Chinese men packed their bags and sailed across the ocean to get rich.

Chinese miners weren't treated like everyone else. Other miners of European ancestry (white men) didn't want the Chinese taking all the gold. They didn't think the Chinese were as good as they were either. So the United States passed the Foreign Miner Tax. Every Chinese miner had to pay a tax to look for gold. People who refused to pay the tax were beaten or even killed.

THE RAILROAD

More and more Chinese were coming to the United States. Many of them worked on the Transcontinental Railroad (a railroad that was built to cross the entire continent of North America, from east to west). Other Americans did not want to do such hard and dangerous work. Chinese workers needed wages, and they didn't have many job choices in this country. They were willing to work hard.

When the Transcontinental Railroad was completed, people celebrated—but no one gave any credit to the Asians who had done much of the labor.

So, anywhere from 9,000 to 12,000 Chinese went to work for the Central Pacific Railroad, building the western part of the Transcontinental Railroad. For all their work, they didn't make much money. They made much less than immigrant workers from Europe did for doing the same jobs. When the Chinese workers went on strike, the railroad refused to feed them until they went back to work, and the strike was unsuccessful. Several hundred Chinese workers died doing this work.

Very few people appreciated that the Transcontinental Railroad was built in large part by Chinese laborers. When talking about the final ceremony marking the end of railroad construction, author Helen Zia writes, "The speeches congratulated European immigrant workers for their labor but never mentioned the Chinese. Instead, Chinese men were summarily fired and forced to walk the long distance back to San Francisco—forbidden to ride on the railroad they built."

ANTI-CHINA

People all over the West distrusted and disliked the Chinese immigrants coming to North America. The Chinese were also visibly different than most people of European ancestry. This meant they could be easily picked out as targets of xenophobia (a word that means "intense fear of foreigners").

In 1882, the U.S. government reacted to people's fear and dislike. They passed the Chinese Exclusion Act. This law banned all Chinese immigration. It also prevented any Chinese immigrants from becoming American citizens; children born to Chinese parents in the United States wouldn't automatically

A political cartoon from 1882 shows a Chinese man being excluded from entry to the "Golden Gate of Liberty."

become citizens either. The Chinese Exclusion Act was later used to restrict the rights of immigrants from other parts of Asia, like India, Korea, and Japan.

Meanwhile, the same things were going on in Canada, especially in the province of British Colombia. Chinese, Japanese and South Asians could not vote, practice law, be elected to public office, serve on juries, or work in public works, pharmacies, education, or the civil service. Many Canadians were against Asian immigration—and they expressed their feelings on several occasions in violent anti-Chinese and anti-Asian riots; the most serious was in Vancouver in 1887 and 1907. People didn't want Asian children going to public schools; they wanted to restrict the sale of land to Asians, and to limit the number of licenses issued to Japanese fishermen.

Throughout North America, Asians were regarded as alien and inferior. People believed that Asians were just too different to ever become part of North American society. Labor unions claimed that Asians took jobs away from whites and lowered living standards for all workers because they were willing to work for less money than white workers. Asians were excluded from most unions, and as a matter of policy, employers paid Asian workers less than they did others.

In the United States, the Chinese Exclusion Act was not **repealed** until 1943. Even then, only a very small number of Asian immigrants were allowed into the country. Americans were not yet ready to accept Asian Americans, even though plenty of people had found a way to get by these harsh laws.

WORLD WAR II

World War II was, to put it mildly, a low point in the treatment of Asian Americans in the United States and Canada. Japanese Americans were specifically targeted during this time period. The United States and Canada were at war with Japan, and many Canadians and Americans didn't trust the Japanese who lived in North America. They thought people who came from Japanese backgrounds would feel more loyalty to Japan than they did to their new homes. Whites looked at Asians (not just Japanese) as potential spies. These feelings were based on fear—but they also disguised simple prejudice and racism.

In 1942, soon after Japan bombed Pearl Harbor, U.S. President Franklin D. Roosevelt ordered that people of Japanese descent be rounded up and placed in internment camps. Over 100,000 people ended up imprisoned. Most of them were actually American citizens. The overcrowded camps were filled with disease, hunger, and boredom. Prisoners had to make statements of loyalty, and some ended up in jail. Unlike the Nazi concentration camps in Germany, the point was not to kill all Japanese Americans, but it was still cruel and unjust.

Meanwhile, in Canada, the government issued an order after Pearl Harbor that all Japanese must leave their homes in the Pacific Coast area. More than 22,000 Japanese Canadians were relocated to the interior of British Colombia and to other provinces. These people had been mostly fishermen, so they

Other Immigrants and World War II

The United States was fighting other countries besides Japan. Did any people from those other countries end up in camps? Yes, actually, but not to the same degree as the Japanese. Italian and German immigrants were interrogated, had restrictions placed on their freedom, and were sometimes sent to relocation camps. However, very few American-born people of Italian or German ancestry were imprisoned. European-born immigrants were tolerated much more than Asian-born immigrants (or other people considered to be a different race). Japanese and Japanese-Americans were treated the most harshly as a group.

no longer had a way to support themselves—and the inland communities did not welcome them either. The government sold their property so they could not even look forward to going back home at the end of the war. Toward the end of the war, the Canadian government also encouraged the Japanese to seek voluntary deportation to Japan, and after the war these deportation plans proceeded.

Many Americans and Canadians knew this was wrong. Civil rights groups worked hard to bring an end to these practices. Eventually, Japanese Canadians received some **reparation** from the government for their property, and the restrictions that prevented Japanese from returning to the Pacific Coast came to an end. In the United States, the camps finally closed in 1946, and the U.S. government later apologized to Japanese Americans and provided reparations.

THE SECOND HALF OF THE TWENTIETH CENTURY

When the United States and Canada joined the United Nations (UN) in the 1940s, they joined a global community. The UN's Universal Declaration of Human Rights was written in 1948— and the United States and Canada were forced to look at their

What Does the United Nations Have to Say?

"The term 'racial discrimination' shall mean any distinction, exclusion, restriction, or preference based on race, colour, descent, or national or ethnic origin that has the purpose or effect of nullifying or impairing the recognition, enjoyment or exercise, on an equal footing, of human rights and fundamental freedoms in the political, economic, social, cultural or any other field of public life."

own discriminatory practices. Asian groups took a stand for their rights, and more and more whites supported them.

But prejudice against Asians continued to exist. And sometimes, tragically, it erupted into violence.

The murder of Vincent Chin in Detroit, Michigan, in 1982 is an example of this. Two white men called him a "jap" (even though he was Chinese American) and blamed him and Japanese automakers for the economic hard times in the United States. The men said it was Vincent's fault that they were about to lose their jobs at a car factory. Vincent tried to

Asians and the Right to Vote

In the United States, Asian Pacific Americans had been considered "aliens ineligible for citizenship" ever since 1790. Changes to the laws in 1943, 1946, and 1952 allowed some but not all immigrant Asian Pacific Americans the right to vote. Because only American citizens can vote, immigrant Asian Pacific Americans did not vote in large numbers until after 1965, when the immigration and naturalization laws were changed.

Meanwhile, in Canada, South Asians and Chinese received the right to vote in 1947, and Japanese in 1949.

run for his life, but the two men caught him, held him down, and beat him to death with a baseball bat.

The Asian community (and many others) were outraged when the courts charged the two men with manslaughter (accidentally killing someone) rather than murder. The men received a $3,700 fine and no jail time. An Asian American pointed out, "You can kill a dog and get thirty days in jail, ninety days for a traffic ticket." Human rights organizations formed a multi-racial coalition to demand justice for the murder of Vincent Chin. They organized rallies and protests, circulated petitions, and kept the issue in the national spotlight. The two men never did serve any prison time for their crime. But the incident did bring to Americans' attention the reality of prejudice against Asians.

Asians have a reputation for being high achievers in the academic world. Although many Asians do in fact value educational achievement, this is another stereotype that can actually contribute to prejudice.

TODAY

Unfortunately, prejudice against Asian Americans is still around today.

In the past few decades, immigrants from all over Asia have come to the United States and Canada. They have raised families and contributed to North American communities.

Jeremy Lin

There are Asian politicians. Many Asian students go to college and get good careers. In general, Asians are an accepted part of U.S. and Canadian society.

However, the recent success of basketball star Jeremy Lin highlights the problems that often lie hidden. Lin is a Harvard graduate who joined the NBA as the first Asian American professional basketball player. His race has become a big topic of conversation, especially in the media.

Some reporters used racial slurs to talk about Lin, who is Taiwanese American. An editor at ESPN was even fired for allowing an especially hurtful headline into the press. At games, fans yelled racial remarks and referenced things like Chinese food.

There is plenty of racism in sports today, and other minorities have struggled for a long time to gain acceptance as players on the field and the court. Asian Americans must also face this struggle, both in sports and in other arenas.

Asian teenagers report being bullied more often than teens of other backgrounds. Asians in both Canada and the United States regularly run into stereotypes. There is even racial violence directed against Asian Americans, such as the 2006 attack in Queens in which white men shouting racial threats beat up four Chinese men. Clearly, sadly, prejudice is still alive and well.

Real-Life Stories

I t's one thing to talk about prejudice and racism. It's another to actually live it and see it in real life. Prejudice against Asians isn't always talked about either. Sometimes it gets buried under other problems the world faces today. The stories that follow show that, unfortunately, Asians still experience prejudice of all kinds.

RACISM IN SCHOOL

In 2009 in Ontario, a fifteen-year-old boy was playing in the gym, when he heard someone yell an insult at him. The boy

Prejudice in high schools can lead to bullying, making life hard for Asian students.

had been born in Asia, but he and his family had lived in Canada for five years. He was a straight-A student, and he usually loved his school—so he was taken by surprise when he found himself being shoved around and called names. A hand shot out and punched him in the face. He had never been in a fight before in his life, but with blood trickling from his mouth, the boy turned to his martial arts training and struck back.

The next thing he knew, the boy found himself in trouble, both with school authorities and the law. Other students at the high school came to his defense, however. Hundreds of students skipped classes to rally against racism and to protest the criminal charges laid against the boy. Ultimately, the boy still had to face disciplinary action at his school for fighting—but criminal charges were dropped.

Facinghistory.org tells another story about an Asian-American student at Stuyvesant High School in New York City. Jeanne Park's story sheds light on how even positive stereotypes of Asians can be hurtful.

Who am I? For Asian-American students, the answer is a diligent, hardworking and intelligent young person. But living up to this reputation has secretly haunted me.

The labeling starts in elementary school. It's not uncommon for a teacher to remark, "You're Asian, you're supposed to do well in math." The underlying message is, "You're Asian and you're supposed to be smarter."

Not to say being labeled intelligent isn't flattering, because it is, or not to deny that basking in the limelight of being top of my class isn't ego-boosting, because frankly it

High schools and colleges that value diversity promote valuable learning experiences. We all have a lot to learn from each other!

is. But at a certain point, the pressure became crushing. I felt as if doing poorly on my next spelling quiz would stain the exalted reputation of all Asian students forever.

So I continued to be an academic overachiever, as were my friends. By junior high school I started to believe I was indeed smarter. I became condescending toward non-Asians. I was a bigot; all my friends were Asians. The thought of intermingling occurred rarely if ever.

My **elitist** opinion of Asian students changed, however, in high school. As a student at what is considered one of the nation's most competitive science and math schools, I found that being on top is no longer an easy feat.

I quickly learned that Asian students were not smarter. How could I ever have believed such a thing? All around me are intelligent, ambitious people who are not only Asian but white, black, and Hispanic.

Superiority complexes aside, the problem of **social segregation** still exists in the schools. With few exceptions, each race socializes only with its "own kind." Students see one another in the classroom, but outside the classroom there remains distinct segregation.

Racist lingo abounds. An Asian student who socializes only with other Asians is believed to be an Asian Supremacist or, at the very least, arrogant and closed off. Yet an Asian student who socializes only with whites is called a "Twinkie," one who is yellow on the outside but white on the inside.

A white teenager who socializes only with whites is thought of as prejudiced, yet one who socializes with Asians is considered an "egg," white on the outside and yellow on the inside.

These **culinary** classifications go on endlessly, needless to say, leaving many confused, and leaving many more

The effects of prejudice are particularly hard on children.

fearful than ever of social experimentation. Because the stereotypes are accepted almost unanimously, they are rarely challenged. Many develop harmful stereotypes of entire races. We label people before we even know them.

Labels learned at a young age later change into more visible acts of racism. . . . We all hold misleading stereotypes of people that limit us as individuals in that we cheat ourselves out of the benefits different cultures can contribute. We can grow and learn from each culture whether it be Chinese, Korean, or African-American.

Just recently some Asian boys in my neighborhood were attacked by a group of young white boys who have christened themselves the Master Race. Rather than being angered by this act, I feel pity for this generation that lives in a state of bigotry.

It may be too late for our parents' generation to accept that each person can only be judged for the characteristics that set him or her apart as an individual. We, however, can do better.

This next story was featured on jadeluckclub.com, and is told by Ying Ma, a Chinese American growing up in a poor neighborhood. He also faced prejudice, but of a different kind. This was even more hateful that the pressure that Jeanne faced.

At age ten, I immigrated from China to Oakland, California, a city filled with crime, poverty, and racial tension. In elementary school, I didn't wear name-brand clothing or speak English. My name soon became "Ching Chong," "China girl," and "Chow Mein." Other children laughed at my language, my culture, my ethnicity, and my race. I said nothing.

After a few years, I began to speak English, but not well enough to trade racial insults. On rides home from school I avoided the back of the bus so as not to be beaten up. But even when I sat in the front, fire crackers, paper balls, small rocks, and profanity were thrown at me and the other "stupid Chinamen." The label "Chinamen" was dished out indiscriminately to Vietnamese, Koreans, and other Asians. When I looked around, I saw that the other "Chinamen" tuned out the insults by eagerly discussing movies, friends, and school.

During my secondary school years, racism, and then the combination of outrage and bitterness that it fosters, accompanied me home on the bus every day. My English was by now more fluent than that of those who insulted me, but most of the time I still said nothing to avoid being beaten up. In addition to everything else thrown at me, a few times a week I was the target of sexual remarks vulgar enough to make Howard Stern blush. When I did respond to the insults, I immediately faced physical threats or attacks, along with the embarrassing fact that the other "Chinamen" around me simply continued their quiet personal conversations without intervening. The reality was that those who cursed my race and ethnicity were far bigger in size than most of the Asian children who sat silently.

These stories highlight the different types of prejudice and racism that Asian students encounter in the United States. Many feel the pressure to do well in school because of their race, and the problems that come with that stereotype. Asian Americans must also deal with hurtful names and even violence all because of their race.

Realizing that prejudice is such a big deal can be upsetting. But it's the first step in the fight against prejudice.

Fighting Prejudice

The United States used to be called a melting pot. This expression meant that people of different races, religions, and ethnic backgrounds had all come together in America. Today, many people think that "melting pot" is the wrong **metaphor** to use for the United States, because it implies that all these different kinds of people cooked down into a single "stew," losing their individual characteristics. Nowadays, people speak instead of the United States as a salad bowl or a mosaic—something where all the separate pieces hold on to what makes them different and special, and yet all of them contribute to something bigger, the thing that makes America what it is today.

Americans and Canadians both, no matter their backgrounds, share some very important beliefs. They believe in democracy, in freedom of speech, and in the right for a person to worship as he chooses. These common beliefs give us an important foundation on which to come together. They give us something to work toward, despite our differences.

President Woodrow Wilson once said that America is not set apart from other countries "so much by its wealth and power as by the fact that it was born with an **ideal**, a purpose." The United States was created to be a nation where the people rule themselves, where everyone has certain rights, regardless of the color of their skin, their religion, their gender, or how much money they have.

AMERICA'S BATTLE AGAINST PREJUDICE

At the very beginning of the United States, when the thirteen original colonies first declared their independence from England on July 4, 1776, they stated that all "are created equal, that they are endowed by their Creator with certain **unalienable** rights, that among them are Life, Liberty, and the pursuit of happiness."

America's history is the story of how it has struggled to live up to these ideals. The Civil War was a part of that struggle. Although the war was fought mostly about black people, its outcome had very important affects on all Americans' rights,

President Woodrow Wilson

especially those of minorities—including Asian Americans'. Near the end of that war, President Abraham Lincoln expressed his belief in the nation's central ideal of freedom for all: "It is not merely for today, but for all time to come. . . . The nation is worth fighting for, to secure such an inestimable jewel."

The Civil Rights Act of 1866 won another small victory in the battle against prejudice, stating that "all persons shall have the same rights . . . to make and enforce contracts, to sue, be parties, give evidence, and to the full and equal benefit of all laws." Then, in 1868, the 14th Amendment made still deeper inroads in the legal battle to live up to America's ideals. This amendment stated that "all persons born or **naturalized** in the United States . . . are citizens . . . nor shall any State deprive any person of life, liberty, or property, without **due process of law**; nor deny to any person . . . the equal protection of the laws."

These changes to American laws were important steps in the fight against prejudice—but in real life, prejudice was still an everyday occurrence. Asian Americans from many countries had to deal with mistreatment and hatred on a daily basis. The Civil Rights Movement of the 1960s continued the struggle, and another major victory was won in 1964, when the Civil Rights Act was passed. It prohibited employment discrimination based on race, sex, national origin, or religion.

Today, both America and Canada are doing a much better job at living up to their ideals than they did two hundred years ago, a hundred years ago, or even fifty years ago. Laws are a good way to protect people's rights and fight prejudice.

But ultimately, prejudice is something that lives inside people. No law can change the way a person thinks about others. That's something we have to do. We do it by changing the way we talk and act. We do it by changing the way we think.

How Many Asian Canadians Are There?

Eleven percent of all Canadians are Asian of some kind. That group can be broken down even more, though. More than a million come from China. About a million are from India. Half a million are from the Philippines. The rest come from Vietnam, Korea, Cambodia, Japan, and many other Asian countries.

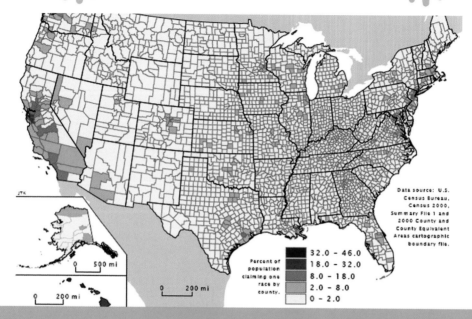

Data source: U.S. Census Bureau, Census 2000, Summary File 1 and 2000 County and County Equivalent Areas cartographic boundary file.

Percent of population claiming one race by county.

32.0 - 46.0
18.0 - 32.0
8.0 - 18.0
2.0 - 8.0
0 - 2.0

This map shows where Asians live in the United States. The darker areas mean that a larger percentage of the population in that region is Asian. Overall, about 5 percent of the American population is Asian, but the percentages are much higher in some areas, especially parts of California and Washington State.

CELEBRATING DIVERSITY

One of the first things that has to change is the way we think about differences. Instead of being frightened of the ways people are different from ourselves, we need to start feeling curious and interested. We need to be willing to learn from people who are different. We need to enjoy the differences!

Most people enjoy diversity when it comes to the world around them. They like different kinds of food. They read different kinds of books. They enjoy different kinds of music and television shows. The world would be pretty boring if everything was exactly the same!

People are also diverse, in the same way as the rest of the world is. Although all of us feel the same basic emotions—sadness and happiness, anger and laughter, loneliness and pride, jealousy and compassion, to name just a few—and most of us have pretty much the same structure—a head, a body, arms and legs—we also are different in many ways. Our hair, eyes, and skin come in different colors. Our noses are big or little or something in between. Our bodies are different sizes and shapes. And when you get down to the details—to our fingerprints and the DNA inside our cells—we're absolutely unique, despite all the things we have in common with other human beings. Each of us looks at the world a little differently. We believe different things. And we offer different things as well.

The world is a richer place because of all this human diversity. You can learn from and enjoy your friends because, although they're like you in some ways, they're also different from you in other ways. Those differences make them interesting! And in a similar way, we can learn from human beings' different languages, different music, different ways of thinking about God, different lifestyles.

Prejudice, however, focuses on the differences in a negative way. It doesn't value all that differences have to offer us. Instead, it divides people into in-groups and out-groups. It breaks the Golden Rule.

Do you recognize prejudice when you hear it? Sometimes it's hard. We get so used to certain ways of thinking that we become blind to what's really going on. But anytime you hear people being lumped together, chances are prejudice is going on. Statements like these are all signs of prejudice:

Poor kids smell bad.
Girls run funny.
Old people are boring.
Special ed kids are weird.
Jocks are jerks.

Rather than building bridges between people, prejudice puts up walls. It makes it hard to talk to others or understand them. And those walls can lead to hatred, violence, and even wars.

What Is the Golden Rule?

"Treat others the way you want to be treated." It's the most basic of all human moral laws—and it's been found in all religions and all cultures for thousands of years. The earliest record of this principle is in the Code of Hammurabi, written nearly 4,000 years ago. About 2,500 years ago, Confucius, the great Chinese philosopher, wrote, "Never impose on others what you would not choose for yourself." An ancient Egyptian papyrus contains a similar thought: "That which you hate to be done to you, do not do to another." Ancient Greek philosophers wrote, "Do not do to others what would anger you if done to you by others." An early Buddhist teacher expressed a similar concept: "Just as I am so are they, just as they are so am I." Jesus Christ, whom Christians follow, said, "Do unto others as you would have them do unto you." The Prophet Mohammed, whose teachings Muslims follow, said, "As you would have people do to you, do to them; and what you dislike to be done to you, don't do to them," as well as, "That which you seek for yourself, seek for all humans."

You can't follow this ancient rule and practice prejudice. The Golden Rule and prejudice are not compatible!

A first step to ending prejudice is speaking up against it whenever you hear it. Point it out when you hear your friends or family being prejudiced. They may not even realize that's what they're being.

Getting to know people is one of the best ways to overcome prejudice.

But even more important, you need to spot prejudice when it's inside you. That's not always easy, of course. Here are some ways experts suggest you can fight prejudice when you find it inside yourself:

1. Learn more about groups of people who are different from you. Read books about their history; read fiction that allows you to walk in their shoes in your imagination; watch movies that portray them accurately.

2. Get to know people who are different from you. Practice being a good listener, focusing on what they have to say rather than on your own opinions and experiences. Ask about others' backgrounds and family stories.

3. Practice compassion. Imagine what it would feel like to be someone who is different from you. Your imagination is a powerful tool you can use to make the world better!

4. Believe in yourself. Surprisingly, a lot of the time, psych- ologists say, prejudice is caused by having a bad self- concept. If you don't like who you are and you don't believe

in your own abilities, you're more likely to be scared and threatened by others. People who are comfortable with themselves are also more comfortable with people who are different from themselves.

What does it all come down to in the end? Perhaps the war against prejudice can best be summed up with just two words: communication and respect.

More Ways to Fight Prejudice

- Be aware of the words you use. Avoid remarks that are based on stereotypes and challenge those made by others.
- Speak out against jokes and slurs that target people or groups. It is not enough to refuse to laugh; silence sends a message that you are in agreement.
- Volunteer to work with agencies that fight prejudice or that work on behalf of minorities in your community.
- Attend local cultural events.
- Eat at ethnic restaurants.

FIND OUT MORE

In Books

Ngai, Mae M. *Impossible Subjects: Illegal Aliens and the Making of Modern America.* Princeton, N.J.: Princeton Press, 2004

Okihiro, Gary Y. *Columbia Guide to Asian American History.* New York: Columbia University Press, 2001

Takaki, Robert. *Strangers from a Different Shore.* New York: Little, Brown, and Company, 2008.

On the Internet

ASIAN AMERICAN ALLIANCE

www.asianamericanalliance.com/Advancing-Equality.html

ASIAN AMERICAN HISTORY

www.pbs.org/ancestorsintheamericas

ASIAN NATION

www.asian-nation.org/racism.shtml

GLOSSARY

culinary: Relating to specific methods of preparing food.

cystic fibrosis: A hereditary disease that causes problems in the lungs.

due process of law: Fair treatment through the court system. In other words, no one can be put in prison without a trial or other legal protection.

effeminate: Possessing feminine qualities; usually applied to males in a negative way.

elitist: Believing that some people are better than others.

genes: The part of our DNA that carries hereditary information from parent to child.

harassment: To attack or intimidate continually.

ideal: An idea about what is perfect.

metaphor: Something that represents another idea.

naturalized: Made a citizen.

oversimplification: The process of making something complicated too simple.

reparation: Money or other help given to those who have been wronged.

repealed: Gotten rid of; usually a law.

sickle cell disease: A blood disease that causes deformed red blood cells.

social segregation: Legally keeping different groups of people apart in public.

sociologists: People who study the way groups of humans behave.

unalienable: Having to do with something that cannot be separated or taken away.

BIBLIOGRAPHY

"Ancestors in the Americas." PBS. April 3, 2012. www.pbs.org/ancestorsintheamericas.

Asian Nation. April 2, 2012. www.asian-nation.org/index.shtml.

"Becoming American: the Chinese Experience." PBS. April 3, 2012. www.pbs.org/becomingamerican.

Clarkson, Brett. "A Blow Against Racism." *The Toronto Sun.* April 28, 2009.

"Exploring the Japanese Internment." April 3, 2012. caamedia.org/jainternment.

Freeman, Hadley. "Jeremy Lin Row Reveals Deep-Seated Racism Against Asian Americans." *The Guardian.* April 3, 2012. www.guardian.co.uk/commentisfree/cifamerica/2012/feb/21/jeremy-lin-racism-asian-americans.

Le, C.N. "The First Asian Americans." *Asian-Nation: The Landscape of Asian America*, April 3, 2012. www.asian-nation.org/first.shtml.

Ma, Ying. "Anti Asian American Racism Perpetrated by Other Minority Groups: Black Racism." November 9, 2011. jadeluckclub.com/fresh-thinking-race-america.

Park, Jeanne. "Letter to the Editor." *New York Times.* April, 20, 1990.

Zia, Helen. *Asian American Dreams: The Emergence of an American People.* New York: Farrar, Straus and Giroux, 2001.

INDEX

Picture Credits

About the Author

Z.B. Hill is a an author and publicist living in Binghamton, New York. He has a special interest in adolescent education.